What's inside

Why read this guide?

Like many people, you may never have been a guardian of someone else's property before. That's why we created *Managing someone else's money: Help for court-appointed guardians of property and conservators*. This guide will help you understand what you can and cannot do in your role as a **guardian**. In that role, you are a **fiduciary**. For this guide, a fiduciary is anyone named to manage money or property for someone else. You'll find brief tips to help you avoid problems and resources for finding more information.

This guide is for family and friends serving as a guardian of property, not for professionals or organizations. The guide does not give you legal advice. State laws vary, so you may have additional duties. Talk to a lawyer if you have questions about your duties.

If you want to learn about how to become a guardian of property, this guide is not designed for you. Talk to a lawyer or read other guides from your state bar association or others.

Let's start with a scenario about how you might have become a guardian of property

Your family member or friend may not be able to make decisions on his own about his money and property. For this guide, let's call him Martin. After a hearing, the court has named you **guardian of property** for Martin. You now have the duty and power to make decisions on Martin's behalf about some or all of his money and property.

The court has given you a lot of responsibility as Martin's guardian of property.

You are now a **fiduciary** with **fiduciary duties**.

What is a fiduciary?

Since you have been named to manage money or property for someone else, you are a **fiduciary**. The law requires you to manage Martin's money and property for HIS benefit, not yours. It does not matter if you are managing a lot of money or a little. It does not matter if you are a family member or not.

The role of a fiduciary carries with it legal responsibilities. When you act as a fiduciary for Martin, you have four basic duties that you must keep in mind:

1. Act only in Martin's best interest.
2. Manage Martin's money and property carefully.
3. Keep Martin's money and property separate from yours.
4. Keep good records.

As a fiduciary, you must be trustworthy, honest, and act in good faith. If you do not meet these standards, you could be removed as a fiduciary, sued, or have to repay money. It is even possible that the police or sheriff could investigate you and you could go to jail. **That's why it's always important to remember: It's not your money!**

Guardian of property questions and answers

What is a guardian of property?

A **guardian of property** is someone the court names to manage money and property for someone else whom the court has found cannot manage it alone.

Sometimes a guardian of property is also appointed as **guardian of the person**. A guardian of the person makes Martin's health care and other personal decisions. Sometimes a different person is appointed to be the guardian of the person, or Martin himself may still be able to make these personal decisions.

This guide only covers duties of the guardian of property. **Terms can differ.** In many states a guardian of property may be called a

Different types of fiduciaries exist

In your role as guardian of property, you may act as or deal with other types of fiduciaries. These may include:

Trustees under a revocable living trust—someone names them to manage money and property.

Representative payees or, for veterans, VA fiduciaries—a government agency names them to manage government money that is paid to someone.

Agents under a power of attorney—someone names an agent to manage their money and property in case they are not able to do it.

Other guides explaining the duties of these fiduciaries are at: www. consumerfinance.gov/ managing-someone-elses- money.

conservator or **guardian of estate**. Martin's money and property is called his **estate**. A person under guardianship may be called an **incapacitated person, protected person** or **ward**.

What are your responsibilities as a guardian of property?

As guardian of property, you have a double duty—both to Martin, the person you are serving, and to the court.

Duty to Martin

You must always keep Martin's best interests in mind. In managing his money, you must act for his good and not for your own good. Involve Martin in decisions as much as possible.

Duty to the Court

You are an agent of the court. The court has trusted you. You must report to the court regularly and be ready to answer any questions.

When do your responsibilities end?

Your responsibilities as Martin's guardian of property last until the court relieves you of your duties. The court may do this because someone else has been appointed, Martin has died, or Martin no longer needs a guardian.

Don't expect others to know what a guardian of property is or does.

They may not understand that you have been appointed by the court. They may think you have more authority or less authority than you really have. You may need to educate them. You could show them this guide and a copy of the court order appointing you.

Four basic duties of a fiduciary

Duty 1 | Act only in Martin's best interest

Because you are dealing with Martin's money and property, your duty is to make decisions that are best for him. This means you must ignore your own interests and needs, or the interests and needs of other people.

To help act in Martin's best interest, follow these guidelines:

- **Read the court order.** Your powers and duties as Martin's guardian of property are written in state law. They also may be written in the court order that appointed you. Some court orders may be detailed, while others may be very general. Read the court order closely, and talk to a lawyer if you don't understand it. In some states, a guardian is required to have a lawyer. Ask questions and learn all you can about what you should do—and what you should not do.

- **Do what the court order says—and don't do what it says you should not do.** It is important that you not act beyond what the law and the court order allow, and that you carry out the basic tasks necessary. Your powers may be limited to certain actions or certain amounts of money. You may need to get the court to approve other actions. Even if you have the best intentions, follow the court order.

- **As much as possible, involve Martin in decisions.** Many things can affect your decisions. For example, you might feel pressure from others. Martin's abilities to make decisions might change from time to time, or maybe Martin was never able to make decisions about his money and property. Consider these three steps:

  - First, ask Martin what he wants. He may be able to decide some things. If so, take this into account, especially if it is similar to his thinking in the past and the risk of harm to him is not unreasonable. For example, if Martin wants to handle money, see if he can manage a small bank account or a monthly cash allowance. Doing this will let him be in charge of a set amount, and you will limit the risk to that amount.

  - Second, try to find out what Martin would have wanted. Look at any past decisions, actions, and statements. Find as much information as you can. Ask people who care about Martin what they think he would have wanted. Make the decision you think that Martin would have made, unless doing so would harm him.

▫ Third, do what you think is best for him. If you have looked hard and still don't know what Martin would have wanted—or if Martin could never make decisions about money and property—use your judgment about what is best. Put Martin's well-being above saving money for others who may inherit his money and property. Make sure that he is safe and comfortable, and his needs are met.

- **Avoid conflicts of interest.** A conflict of interest happens if you make a decision about Martin's property that may benefit someone else at Martin's expense. Because you were appointed by the court, you have a strict duty to avoid conflicts of interest—or even the appearance of a conflict of interest. Try to keep an "arm's length distance" between your interests and any use of Martin's money.

- **Don't borrow, loan, or give Martin's money to yourself or others.** Even if the court order clearly allows gifts to you or others, be very careful to avoid conflicts of interest. Usually, the court must approve gifts or loans, or those over a certain amount. Make sure that any gifts do not increase or complicate Martin's taxes or change his plans for his property when he dies. Any gifts or loans should be in line with what Martin would have wanted. For example, if Martin gave money every year to a charity, the court may allow you to continue doing that.

- **Avoid changing Martin's plans for giving away his money or property when he dies.** There may be rare situations when changing Martin's plans is in his best interest. But you should get legal advice and approval from the court before you do anything.

- **Don't pay yourself for the time you spend acting as Martin's guardian of property, unless the court allows you to do so.** If you are allowed to pay yourself, get legal advice, check with the court, and carefully document how much time you spend and what you do.

To avoid any surprises or misunderstandings, tell family about

Avoid possible conflicts of interest

Sometimes people have good intentions, but do things they shouldn't. Because you are now a fiduciary, you should avoid any conflicts of interest. Here are a few examples of possible conflicts of interest:

Whose car is it?

You used Martin's money to buy a car. You use it to drive him to appointments, but most of the time you drive the car just for your own needs. This may be a conflict of interest.

Should you do business with family?

Martin needs repair work in his apartment. You hire your son and pay him from Martin's money. This may be a conflict of interest, even though the work was needed. It appears that you have put your personal interest to benefit your son in conflict with Martin's interests.

your fees when you begin your duties as a guardian of property. Don't charge fees that are overly high, and don't charge for things you do that are not specifically as guardian of property. For instance, don't charge fees if you shop for Martin or personally make home repairs. If necessary, you can pay someone else at a lower rate for these tasks and document the expenses.

Duty 2 | Manage Martin's money and property carefully

As Martin's guardian of property, you might pay bills, oversee bank accounts, or pay for things he needs. You might also make investments, pay taxes, collect rent or unpaid debts, get insurance if needed, cancel any unneeded insurance, and do other things in the court order.

You have a duty to manage Martin's money and property very carefully. Use good judgment and common sense. As a fiduciary, you must be even more careful with Martin's money than you might be with your own!

Follow these guidelines strictly according to the court's procedures:

- **Make an inventory.** To make careful decisions, you need to know what Martin owns and owes. To make a proper inventory, you must find and list for the court all of Martin's income and property, as well as any debts or legal claims against his properties (called liens.) The court may give you a form and a deadline for making the inventory—for example, you might have 3 months. To avoid any risk to Martin's money and property, you must make the inventory as quickly as possible.

  An inventory may include all kinds of property. Your list might include:

  - Checking and savings accounts;

  - Cash;

  - Pension, retirement, annuity, rental, public benefit, or other income;

  - Real estate;

Tips for making an inventory

Don't leave anything out. Even if you know Martin wants you to have certain things and says so in his will, list them in the inventory. A proper inventory lists everything according to the court's rules. Do not decide that some things should not be listed.

Search carefully. Look carefully to find everything Martin owns. Search his mail and home. Look for real estate by talking to family or advisors and looking through land records. Track down letters from creditors to find unpaid debts. Take valuable items to an appraiser.

Verify if necessary. It is a good idea to have someone else check the list, especially if family might argue over Martin's money and property.

- Cars and other vehicles;

- Insurance policies;

- Trusts for which Martin is a beneficiary;

- Stocks and bonds;

- Jewelry, furniture, and any other items of value; and

- Unpaid credit card bills and other outstanding loans.

- **File the inventory with the court.** Keep a copy of the inventory for your records and file it with the court by the due date. Be ready to share it with family listed with the court as interested parties. In some states, you must have a lawyer review and sign the inventory.

- **The court will probably require you to buy a bond.** The court may require you to buy a bond. A bond is a special type of insurance policy so the court can make sure you carry out your duties. If you fail in your duties and, as a result, money is lost or stolen, the bonding company will pay the money back. Then the company will try to collect the money from you. The cost of the bond may be payable from Martin's money. Ask the court staff whether you may use Martin's money to cover this expense.

  Only people with good financial records and credit histories can get a bond. If you have had a bankruptcy, you will not likely be able to get a bond. Try to check this before you are appointed as guardian of property or as soon as possible. Take all steps the court advises about getting a bond.

  Sometimes, instead of requiring a bond, the court will limit the amount of funds you can take out of Martin's account. This is called a restricted account. The court will tell the bank to block the account above a certain amount. If you want to spend more than that amount, you must get the court to approve the expense.

- **Protect Martin's property.** Keep his money and property safe. Have Martin's income and bills sent to you. Put his valuable items in safe deposit boxes and lock other items he is not using in storage. Keep Martin's cash in bank accounts that earn interest if possible and that have low or no fees. Review bank and other financial statements promptly. If Martin will not be living in his home, consider changing the locks. Figure out if the house should be rented, or how to keep it safe if it is vacant. If Martin rented an apartment and will be moving, tell the landlord, remove his things, and have the apartment cleaned.

- **Make a financial plan.** Make a budget as if you were making one for your own household. List how much you expect to pay for nursing home, assisted living or home care, rent, food, medical care, and home maintenance or repair. Be sure to include a monthly amount for Martin to use as he pleases. Think about any special expenses that may arise, such as dental work or any medical care or equipment that Medicare, Medicaid, or other health insurance will not cover. Try to stick to your budget. If something very costly occurs, you may need the court to approve the expense.

- **Invest carefully.** If you are making investments for Martin, talk to a financial professional. The Securities and Exchange Commission (SEC) provides tips on choosing a financial professional at www.sec.gov/investor/alerts/ib_top_tips.pdf. Discuss your choices and goals for investing based on Martin's needs and values.

- **Pay bills and taxes on time.**

- **Cancel any insurance policies that Martin does not need.**

- **Collect debts.** Find out if anyone owes Martin money, and try to collect it.

- **There's no place like home.** Your state's law or the court order may not allow you to sell Martin's real estate. In any case, it is good practice to get court approval to sell, mortgage, or lease any property.

  Martin may want to continue to live in the home he owns or rents. In that case, take these steps:

  - **Determine if living in his home is safe, and if Martin can manage in the house.** If needed, put in guard rails, grab bars, smoke detectors, extra lighting, and other things to help him stay at home. Tax credits or deductions might be available if you make the home easier to live in. Work with any other decision-makers (such as an agent under a health care power of attorney or any guardian of the person if you have not been appointed to fill this role).

If it is not safe to live at home even with changes—or if Martin wants to move—**consider other places that meet Martin's needs. Try to keep him connected to people and things important to him.** Choices might be living with someone else, or living in a retirement community, a senior apartment, group home, assisted living, or nursing home. You may need court approval for a move.

Can Martin get any benefits?

Find out if Martin is eligible for any financial or health care benefits from an employer or a government. These benefits might include pensions, disability, Social Security, Medicare, Medicaid, Veterans benefits, housing assistance, or food stamps (now known as Supplemental Nutrition Assistance Program or SNAP). Use the National Council on Aging benefits check-up at www.BenefitsCheckUp.org.

Help him apply for those benefits. The Area Agency on Aging where Martin lives can help you find information. Find the local Area Agency on Aging through the Eldercare Locator at www.eldercare.gov.

Medicaid is complicated

Get legal advice and be very careful about decisions that may affect Martin's eligibility for Medicaid. The Medicaid program provides medical assistance and long-term care to low-income people. It may have another name in your state. To find your state Medicaid agency, visit: www.benefits.gov/benefits/browse-by-category/category/MED.

Duty 3 | Keep Martin's money and property separate

Never mix Martin's money or property with your own or someone else's. Mixing money or property makes it unclear who owns what. Confused records can get you in trouble with the court.

Follow these guidelines:

- **Separate means separate.** Never deposit Martin's money into your own or someone else's bank account or investment account.

- **Avoid joint accounts.** If Martin already has money in a joint account with you or someone else, get legal advice before making any change.

- **Keep title to Martin's money and property in his own name.** This is so other people can see right away that the money and property is Martin's and not yours. Ask the bank for a guardianship or fiduciary account that shows you are managing the account for Martin.

- **Know how to sign as guardian.** Sign all checks and other documents relating to Martin's money or property to show that you are Martin's guardian. For example, you might sign: "Juan Doe, as guardian for Martin Roe." Never just sign "Martin Roe."

- **Pay Martin's expenses from his funds, not yours.** Spending your money and then paying yourself back makes it hard to keep good records. If you really need to use your money, save receipts for the expense and keep a good record of why, what, and when you paid yourself.

Duty 4 | Keep good records and report to the court

You must keep true and complete records of Martin's money and property.

As guardian of property, the court or a lawsuit can challenge you to show everything you've done with Martin's money and property. Always be ready to share your records with family—unless you think they will misuse the information to harm Martin.

Practice good recordkeeping habits:

- **Keep a detailed list of everything that you receive or spend for Martin.** Records should include the amount of checks written or deposited, dates, reasons, names of people or companies involved, and other important information.

- **Keep receipts and notes, even for small expenses.** For example, write "$50, groceries, ABC Grocery Store, May 2" in your records soon after you spend the money.

- **Avoid paying in cash.** Try not to pay Martin's expenses with cash. Also, try not to use an ATM card to withdraw cash or write checks to "Cash." If you need to use cash, be sure to keep receipts or notes.

- **Getting paid?** If you are permitted by the court to charge a fee to serve as guardian of property, be sure you charge a reasonable fee. Keep detailed records as you go along of what work you did, how much time it took, when you did it, and why you did it.

- **File your accountings with the court.** Each year—or whenever the court requires—you must report to the court, including giving an accounting of all the money you received and spent.

  - The court will give you a specific form for the accounting or will tell you what is required. Use the records you have kept during the year to fill in the form. If you have questions, ask court staff or a lawyer for help.

- ▫ The court will tell you when the accounting is due. Be sure to turn it in on time. If your accounting is late, the court may call you in to explain why.

- ▫ Your accounting must be clear and must "add up." The accounting should show a beginning balance, income during the year, expenses during the year, and an ending balance. The ending balance for one year should be the same as the beginning balance for the next year.

- ▫ Accounting requirements differ by court, and may change over time. Try to understand in advance what is needed, so that your accounting is not rejected for a minor problem. Ask for an example of a correct accounting. You may need an accountant to help.

- **File a final accounting after Martin dies.** Notify the court when Martin dies. According to court procedures, make a final accounting of Martin's money and property, and ask for an order releasing you from your duties.

  - ▫ Sometimes, you may need to pay final bills or make final arrangements, especially if no one else can do it. For example, you may need to pay funeral expenses and final medical bills.

  - ▫ If Martin did not already make funeral or burial arrangements, look for any directions he may have left–perhaps in advance directives or remarks to family or friends.

  - ▫ An executor named in a will, an administrator named by the court, or a trustee named in a trust will handle Martin's money and property after you turn them over. Hold Martin's personal things safely until they are transferred to whoever is to receive them. If you are the one named to handle Martin's money and property after his death, make sure you understand when your duties as guardian end and your new duties begin.

More things you should know

What if there are other fiduciaries?

Co-guardians

The court may have named someone else to act with you as Martin's guardian of property, or it may have named someone else to act as Martin's guardian of person to make healthcare and other personal decisions.

Any other guardians will be your partners in making decisions on Martin's behalf and in helping him make decisions if he is able. You must work closely together. For example, if Martin will move to a new location or get special care, his guardians must make important personal and financial decisions. You must consult with one another.

Other types of fiduciaries

Other fiduciaries may have authority to make decisions for Martin. For example, he may have an agent under a power of attorney, a representative payee who handles Social Security benefits, or a VA fiduciary who handles veterans benefits. It is important to work with these other fiduciaries, and keep them informed.

Government benefits require special fiduciaries

As guardian of property, you cannot manage Martin's government benefits such as Social Security or VA benefits unless you get a separate appointment from the government agency as, for example, a representative payee or VA fiduciary. For more information, contact the government agency.

How can you avoid problems with family or friends?

Family or friends may not agree with your decisions about Martin's money and property. To help reduce any friction, follow the four duties described above and the guidelines we've given you.

- Sharing information may help (unless Martin has said that you should not). It usually is easier to deal with questions about a decision when it happens than to deal with suspicion and anger that may build over a long time. State law or the court may require you to send accountings to family and friends, or may say you should not. If there is no direction from the court, get court approval before sharing information.

- Some family or friends may not have Martin's best interest at heart, so it may be better not to share information with them, or to ask the court not to share it. Use your best judgment.

- If family or friends don't agree with your decisions, try to get someone to help sort it out—for example, a family counselor or mediator. See *Where to go for help* on page 26 of this guide.

What should you know about working with professionals?

In managing Martin's affairs, you may need help from professionals such as lawyers, brokers, financial advisors, accountants, real estate agents, appraisers, psychologists, social workers, doctors, nurses, or care managers. You can pay them with Martin's money.

If you need help from any professionals, remember these tips:

- **Check on the professional's qualifications.** Many professionals must be licensed or registered by a government agency. Check credentials with the government agency. Make sure the license or registration is current and the professional is in good standing. Check the person's complaint history.

- **Interview the professional thoroughly and ask questions.**

- **Review contracts carefully before signing.** Before hiring any professionals, get their proposed plan of work and expected fee.

- **Make your own decisions based on facts and advice.** Listen to their advice but remember you are the decision-maker.

Watch out for financial exploitation

Family, friends, neighbors, caregivers, fiduciaries, business people, and others may try to take advantage of Martin. They may take his money without permission, neglect to repay money they owe, charge him too much for services, or just not do things he has paid them to do. These may be examples of financial exploitation or financial abuse. As Martin's guardian of property, you should help protect him. You should know the signs of financial exploitation for five important reasons:

1. Martin may still control some of his funds and could be exploited;

2. Even if Martin does not control any of his funds, he still may be exploited;

3. Martin may have been exploited already, and you may still be able to do something about that;

4. People may try to take advantage of you as Martin's guardian; and

5. Knowing what to look for will help you avoid doing things you should not do, protecting you from claims that you have exploited Martin.

Look for these common signs of financial exploitation

- **Some money or property is missing.**

- **Martin says that some money or property is missing.**

- **You notice sudden changes in Martin's spending or savings.** For example, he:

    □ Takes out lots of money from the bank without explanation;

    □ Tries to wire large amounts of money;

    □ Uses the ATM a lot;

    □ Is not able to pay bills that are usually paid;

    □ Buys things or services that don't seem necessary;

    □ Puts names on bank or other accounts that you do not recognize or that he is unwilling or unable to explain;

- Does not get bank statements or bills;

- Makes new or unusual gifts to family or others, such as a "new best friend";

- Changes beneficiaries of a will, life insurance, or retirement funds; or

- Has a caregiver, friend, or relative who suddenly begins handling his money.

- **Martin says he is afraid or seems afraid of a relative, caregiver, or friend.**

- **A relative, caregiver, friend, or someone else keeps Martin from having visitors or phone calls, or does not let him speak for himself, or seems to be controlling his decisions.**

What can you do if Martin has been exploited?

- Call the emergency 911 number if Martin is in immediate danger.

- Call local adult protective services or the police or sheriff. You may be required by law to do this.

- Alert Martin's bank or credit card company.

- Call the local prosecutor or state attorney general.

- Call the long-term care ombudsman program or the state Medicaid fraud control unit if Martin is in a nursing home or assisted living.

- Consider talking to a lawyer about protecting Martin from more exploitation or getting back money or property taken from him.

Each agency or professional has a different role, so you may need to call more than one. For more information, see *Where to go for help* on page 26 of this guide.

Be on guard for consumer scams

As Martin's guardian of property, you should be alert to protect his money from consumer scams as well as financial exploitation. Criminals and con artists have many scams, and change them all the time. They often seek unsuspecting people who have access to money. Learn to spot consumer scams against Martin—and against you as his guardian.

How can you protect Martin from scams?

Consumer scams happen on the phone; through the mail, e-mail, or the Internet; and they occur in person, at home, or at a business.

Here are some tips:

- **Put Martin's number on the National Do Not Call Registry.** Go to www. donotcall.gov or call 1-888-382-1222.

- **Don't share numbers or passwords for Martin's accounts, credit cards, or Social Security,** unless you know whom you're dealing with and why they need the information.

- **After hearing a sales pitch, take time to compare prices.** Ask for information in writing and read it carefully.

- **Too good to be true?** Ask yourself why someone is trying so hard to give you a "great deal." If it sounds too good to be true, it probably is.

- **Watch out for deals that are only "good today" and that pressure you to act quickly.** Be suspicious if you are not given enough time to read a contract or get legal advice before signing. Also watch out if you are told that you need to pay the seller quickly, for example by wiring the money or sending it by courier.

- **Never pay up front for a promised prize.** Suspect a scam if you are required to pay fees or taxes to receive a prize or other financial windfall.

- **Watch for signs Martin already has been scammed.** For example, does he receive a lot of mail or e-mail for sweepstakes? Has he paid people you don't know, especially in other states or countries? Has he taken a lot of money out of the bank while he was with someone he recently met? Does he have a hard time explaining how he spent that money? Is he suddenly unable to pay for food, medicine, or utilities?

What can you do if Martin has been scammed?

If you suspect a scam, get help. Contact a local, state, or federal agency, depending on the type of scam. You may also need to talk to a lawyer.

Local agencies to call are adult protective services, the long-term care ombudsman program, the police or sheriff, and the local Better Business Bureau.

State agencies to call are the office of the attorney general or another agency that deals with consumer protection.

Call a federal agency if scammers are in other states or countries. Federal agencies are the Consumer Financial Protection Bureau, the FBI, the Federal Trade Commission, or the U.S. Postal Inspection Service.

Each of these agencies and professionals has a different role so you may need to call more than one.

For more information, see *Where to go for help* on page 26 of this guide.

Common Consumer Scams

Relative in need	Someone who pretends to be a family member or friend calls or e-mails you to say they are in trouble and need you to wire money right away.
Charity appeals	You get a call or letter from someone asking for money for a fake charity—either the charity does not exist or the charity did not call or write to you.
Lottery or sweepstakes	You get a call or e-mail that you have a chance to win a lot of money through a foreign country's sweepstakes or lottery. The caller will offer tips about how to win if you pay a fee or buy something. Or the caller or e-mail says you already have won and you must give your bank account information or pay a fee to collect your winnings.
Home improvement	Scammers take money for repairs and then they never return to do the work or they do bad work. Sometimes they break something to create more work or they say that things need work when they don't.
Free lunch	Scammers invite you to a free lunch and seminar, and then pressure you to give them information about your money, and to invest the money with them. They offer you "tips" or "guaranteed returns."
Free trip	Scammers say you've won a free trip but they ask for a credit card number or advance cash to hold the reservation.
Government money	You get a call or letter that seems to be from a government agency. Scammers say that if you give a credit card number or send a money order, you can apply for government help with housing, home repairs, utilities, or taxes.
Drug plans	Scammers pretend they are with Medicare prescription drug plans, and try to sell Medicare discount drug cards that are not valid. Companies with Medicare drug plans are not allowed to send unsolicited mail, emails, or phone calls.
Identity theft	Scammers steal personal information—such as a name, date of birth, Social Security number, account number, and mother's maiden name—and use the information to open credit cards or get a mortgage in someone else's name.
Fake "official" mail	Scammers send letters or e-mails that look like they are from a legitimate bank, business, or agency to try to get your personal information or bank account number.

Where to go for help

Local and state agencies

Adult Protective Services

Find the state or local agencies that receive and investigate reports of suspected elder or adult abuse, neglect, or exploitation by contacting the national Eldercare Locator.

1-800-677-1116
www.eldercare.gov

Area Agency on Aging/Aging and Disability Resource Center

Find the local agencies that can give you information about aging and disability services and whether there are any support groups for fiduciaries or caregivers by contacting the national Eldercare Locator.

1-800-677-1116
www.eldercare.gov

Attorney General

Find a listing of state attorneys general on the website of the National Association of Attorneys General. Attorneys general can take action against consumer fraud.

www.naag.org

Better Business Bureau

Find a state or local bureau on the website of the national Better Business Bureau. The BBB can help consumers with complaints against businesses.

www.bbb.org

Long-Term Care Ombudsman Program

Find state and local advocates for residents of long-term care facilities by contacting the national Eldercare Locator.

1-800-677-1116
www.eldercare.gov

Mediators

Find a listing of local mediators on the website of the national Association for Conflict Resolution. Mediation can help resolve disputes and may sometimes be an alternative to legal action.

www.acrnet.org *(Click on "Membership," then "Membership Directory," then "Search")*

Medicaid/Medical Assistance

Find a listing of state agencies that provide Medicaid/Medical Assistance on the federal Benefits.gov website.

www.benefits.gov/benefits/browse-by-category/category/MED

Medicaid Fraud Control Unit

Find a listing of state units on the website of the National Association of Medicaid Fraud Control Units. These units investigate and prosecute abuse and fraud by health care providers.

www.namfcu.net

Police or Sheriff

Find a law enforcement agency by checking the local directory.

Federal agencies

Numerous federal agencies play a role in combatting fraud and abuse and educating consumers. Contact them for more information.

Consumer Financial Protection Bureau
1-855-411-CFPB
www.consumerfinance.gov

Do Not Call Registry
1-888-382-1222
www.donotcall.gov

Federal Bureau of Investigation
www.fbi.gov/scams-safety

Federal Trade Commission
1-877-FTC-HELP (382-4357)
www.consumer.ftc.gov

Financial Fraud Enforcement Task Force
www.stopfraud.gov

Postal Inspection Service
1-877-876-2455
www.postalinspectors.uspis.gov

Social Security Administration
1-800-772-1213
www.socialsecurity.gov/payee

Department of Veterans Affairs
1-888-407-0144
www.benefits.va.gov/fiduciary

For legal help

Free legal services for people over age 60

Find local programs that provide free legal help to people over age 60 by contacting the national Eldercare Locator.

1-800-677-1116
www.eldercare.gov

Free legal services for low-income people

Find local programs that provide free legal help to low-income people on the website of the Legal Services Corporation.

www.lsc.gov/find-legal-aid

Fee-for-service lawyers

This is a web page sponsored by the American Bar Association. It provides information about how to find a lawyer in each state. It also has information about legal resources available in each state, how to check whether a lawyer is licensed, and what to do if you have problems with a lawyer.

www.findlegalhelp.org

For accounting help

Accountants

Find a local certified public accountant on the website of the American Institute of CPAs.

www.aicpa.org/ForThePublic/FindACPA/Pages/FindACPA.aspx

www.ingramcontent.com/pod-product-compliance
Lightning Source LLC
Chambersburg PA
CBHW081811280526
45789CB00008B/3098